Collins Scottish History

WALLACE, BRUCE AND THE WARS OF INDEPENDENCE 1286–1328

Sydney Wood

Collins Educational
An Imprint of HarperCollins*Publishers*

Published by Collins Educational
An imprint of HarperCollins *Publishers* Ltd
77–85 Fulham Palace Road
Hammersmith
London W6 8JB

The HarperCollins web address is:
www.**fire**and**water**.com

First published 1999
Reprinted 2000

ISBN 0 00 327128 5

British Library Cataloguing in Publication Data
A catalogue record for this publication is available from the British Library.

www.**Collins**Education.com
On-line Support for Schools and Colleges

Acknowledgements
p.7: (Bruce and de Bohun)
Eric H M Robertson (1887–1941)/The Bridgeman Art Library
p.17: (John Balliol doing homage to Edward I)
By permission of the British Library
p.21: (William Wallace by Sir George Jamesone)
Private collection
p.23: (Battle of Bannockburn)
By permission of the British Library
p.24: (Battle of Stirling Bridge by Sir William Hole)
Scottish National Portrait Gallery
p.30: (f.7 Robert Bruce with his first wife, the daughter of the Earl of Mar, 1306)
The National Library of Scotland, Edinburgh/The Bridgeman Art Library
p35: (Bruce and de Bohun)
Eric H M Robertson (1887–1941)/The Bridgeman Art Library
p.39: (Arbroath Abbey)
Edinburgh Photographic Library
p.41: (second seal of Robert I)
Courtesy of the National Archives of Scotland
p.43: (statue of William Wallace)
Scotland in Focus Picture Library
p.44: (Wallace memorial)
Edinburgh Photographic Library
p.44: (statue of Robert the Bruce, Bannockburn)
Edinburgh Photographic Library

Edited by Joanne Stone
Design and typesetting by Derek Lee
Map artwork by Chartwell Illustrators
Illustrations by Margaret McKenna
Production by Anna Pauletti
Printed by Scotprint

Contents

Timeline

1286 King Alexander III is killed by a fall from his horse.

1289 The **Treaty of Salisbury**: Margaret 'The Maid of Norway', heiress to the Scottish throne, is to come to Scotland under the protection of King Edward I of England.

1290 The **Treaty of Birgham**: Margaret is to marry Edward I's son.

1290 Margaret dies on her way to Scotland.

1292 Edward I is invited to choose between rival claimants. He selects John Balliol as the next Scottish King.

1294 War between England and France: Edward I asks the Scots to help him.

1295 King John is overthrown by Scottish leaders hostile to Edward I and the English. Scotland signs alliance with France.

1296 Edward attacks Scotland. Town of Berwick sacked by English army. Scots defeated at Dunbar. Balliol surrenders to Edward.

1297 Uprising against Edward's domination of Scotland led by William Wallace and Andrew Murray. **Battle of Stirling Bridge**: Wallace and Murray's army defeats the English.

1298 Wallace appointed as Guardian of the Realm. **Battle of Falkirk**, English army defeats Wallace.

1305 Wallace captured, tried, and executed by Edward I.

1306 Murder of John Comyn by Robert Bruce. Bruce is crowned at Scone, 25 March, as Robert I. Bruce is defeated by Scots hostile to him and by the English.

1307–9 Bruce leads successful guerilla campaign. 1307 Edward I dies, Edward II becomes King.

1309–13 Bruce captures a series of English-held strongholds.

1314 Battle of Bannockburn, 23–24 June. Bruce defeats Edward II's English Army.

1315–18 Edward Bruce campaigns in Ireland and is killed at Dundalk.

1315–23 Bruce launches raids on the North of England.

1320 The **Declaration of Arbroath**: a group of nobles declares that Scotland has been independent for a long time and should not be subject to the English King.

1322 Edward II is deposed. Edward III becomes King.

1328 **Treaty of Edinburgh**: English recognition of Scottish independence. The Pope recognises it too.

1329 Death of Robert I.

Introduction

This book deals with events that happened around 700 years ago. It describes violent and bloodthirsty times when Scotland was a very different place from today. Yet what happened in those distant days still matters. Indeed modern statues have been put up to some people who appear in this book, and films have been made about them. Without the actions of people 700 years ago, like William Wallace, Robert Bruce and their supporters, the idea of Scotland as an independent country might not exist now. Understanding the time of Wallace and Bruce is part of what it means to be Scottish today.

This book is divided into five main chapters:

- *1 A Struggle to Live: A Struggle to Rule* explores **what Scotland was like** at the end of the thirteenth century including how the country was ruled.
- *2 Edward I Takes Control* deals with **a huge crisis in Scottish government**, a crisis that allowed the King of England, Edward I, to become involved in Scottish affairs.
- *3 William Wallace's Astonishing Life* investigates **how Edward I tried to win control of Scotland** and how some Scots, especially **William Wallace**, resisted this and were, for a short while, successful.
- *4 Robert Bruce and Resistance* explains how **Robert Bruce became the Scottish King** and how he eventually defeated English attempts to control Scotland.
- *5 King Robert's Triumph* deals with **how he secured his kingdom**. And finally the *postscript* describes how the **events of this time are still remembered** today.

Certain themes run through the book. Key themes to think about are:

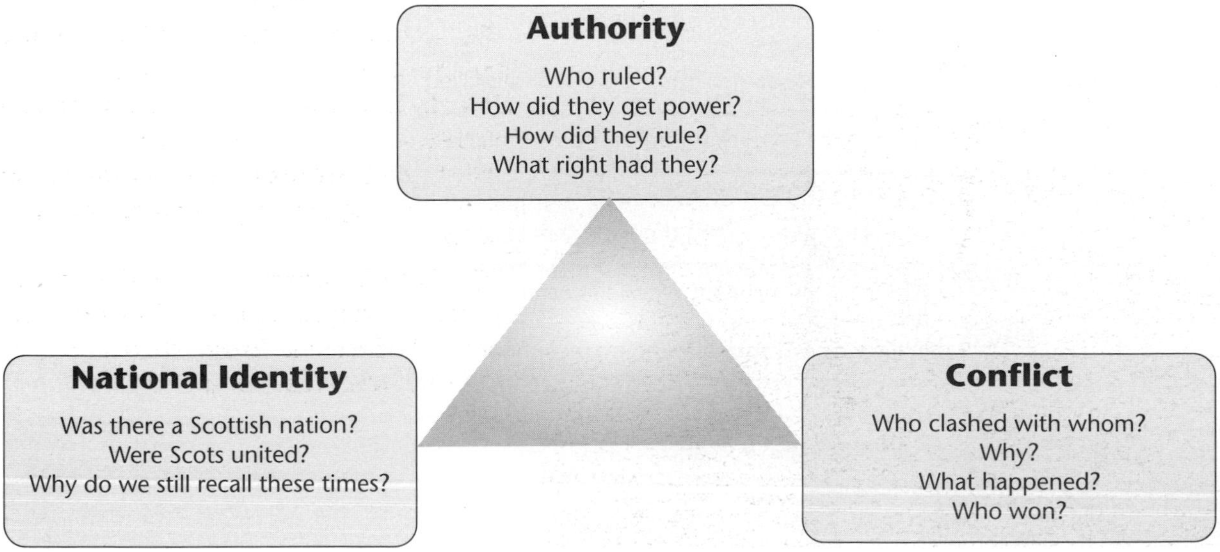

This is a history book. It provides both knowledge and understanding of the past and insights into how we know about the past in several ways.

Information

This comes in:
- Brief lists of key points
- Text
- Diagrams
- Maps
- Illustrations

Sources of historical evidence

These may be:
- Views about the past written many centuries ago
- Historians' views
- Drawings and paintings from the past
- Photos of old objects and buildings
- Old illustrations

There are **activities** in the book to test and develop your historical skills. Can you:

- Show your knowledge and understanding of historical developments, events and issues using knowledge that's relevant and accurate?
- Explain historical developments and events in an organised way using accurate and relevant information?
- Evaluate historical sources showing that you have thought about:
  - their origin or purpose?
  - their content?
  - their context?
  - comparisons between sources?

In each chapter you will find questions to help you think about what you have read.

STOP AND THINK

STOP AND THINK ***Raises questions for you to discuss***

At the end of each chapter is a section for you to practise your skills with questions based on primary sources, which need a more detailed response. Throughout the book the question is raised of how reliable the historical sources are.

The picture on the left shows Robert Bruce fighting a knight from the English army. It was painted by Eric Harold Macbeth Robertson who lived 1887–1941 so .... ***Is it accurate?***

What questions would you want to answer before accepting this as an accurate or helpful source?

This is an important matter to think about. Not many sources have survived from the actual times of Wallace and Bruce. Many were produced later. ***What is safe to trust?***

Scotland – a difficult country to control

The Northern Isles were not part of Scotland but were ruled by the King of Norway.

The Western Isles had only just become part of Scotland (1266).

Mountainous areas were difficult to cross and very difficult to rule over.

Lowland areas were split into sections by rivers and mountains.

This area was the centre of royal power. It had good farmland, several burghs and trade with other countries.

The Borders suffered most in wars between the Scots and the English.

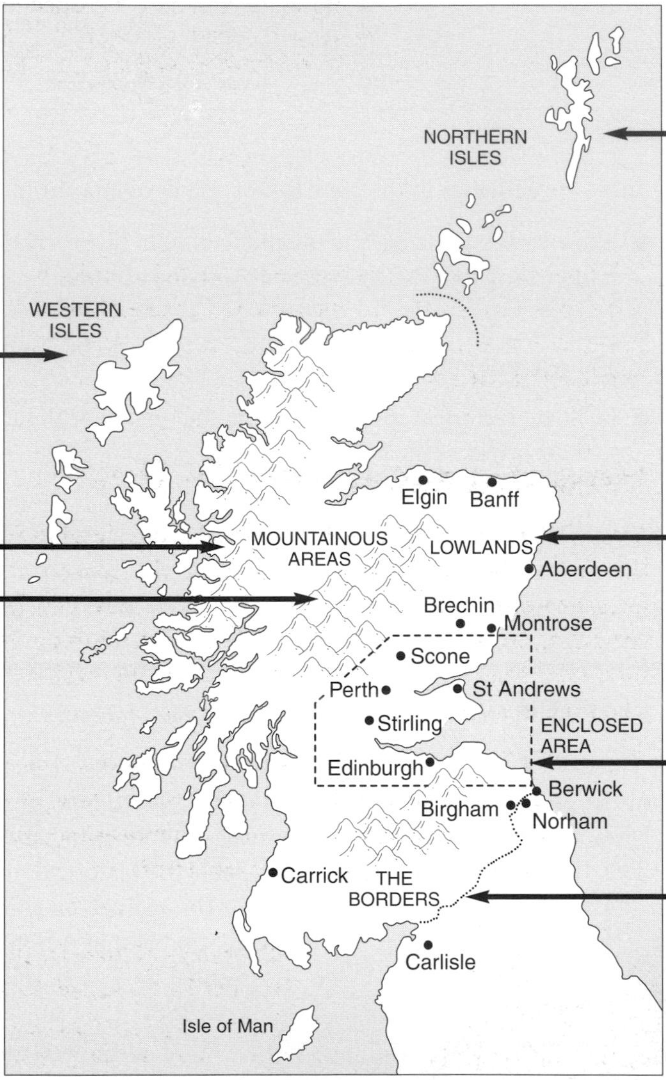

Scotland had been settled by many different peoples: the Celtic Picts in the east, the Irish Scots in the west, Anglo-Saxons in the south east, Britons in the south west, Vikings in the Islands and the far north, and French in the southern area.

'Scotland was a melting pot of peoples.'

(Bruce Webster, historian)

1 A Struggle to Live: A Struggle to Rule

Key Points
This chapter looks at:
- What daily life was like in Scotland 700 years ago.
- How powerful people shaped ordinary people's lives.
- Why the death of King Alexander III in 1286 created such a problem for Scotland.

This book describes events that happened between 1286 and 1329. This was during a period often called 'the middle ages' (or 'medieval period') which stretches from the eleventh to the end of the fifteenth century. Scotland then was a very different place from Scotland today.

How did most people live?

Around 700 years ago fewer than 500,000 people lived in Scotland, just 10 per cent of the size of the population today. Most of the country was either covered in dark forests or large areas of wet and boggy soil. Most people lived in the countryside, struggling to scrape a living by endless hours of work. They rarely travelled more than a few miles from the little clusters of homes where they lived. John of Fordun, who lived in medieval Scotland, wrote:

> *The country is difficult and hard to travel over. To a man on horseback the hills are impassable, save here and there. The woods are full of deer and other woodland beasts. The land of the SEABOARD is fairly level and fertile.*

◆ SEABOARD – land by the coast

Most homes, like this one, were small and simple buildings made from local materials.

The people of these fertile lowland areas grew oats, a kind of barley called 'bere' and kail (a form of cabbage). They kept hens and pigs, and a few cattle. This gave them a diet of porridge, oatcakes and barley bread, cabbage, broth and sometimes milk, cheese and even a little meat and fish. They used very simple tools of wood and iron made by local craftsmen, such as heavy wooden ploughs (each dragged by around a dozen cattle), sickles for cutting corn, and wooden sticks (or flails) for beating the seed heads off the stalks. It was important that all members of a family worked, whatever their age. Few people in medieval Scotland could read and write.

◆ BURGH – place larger than township, often local centres for merchants and craftsmen

◆ BURGESS – important man in the burgh

◆ CHARTER – a written law or statement from a king

To us today no place in thirteenth-century Scotland would seem big enough to be called a town. Even Edinburgh had only four or five hundred houses in it. The larger places were called 'BURGHS'. They had good farmland around them and were mainly on the eastern side of the country by rivers or the coast. Travel in medieval Scotland was very difficult, so moving goods for sale often took place by boat on rivers like the Tay, and at sea. The merchants of Scottish burghs traded with other countries of Northern Europe and with England, bringing in cloth and wine that only the small number of better-off people could afford. Craftsmen like tailors, potters, weavers and metalworkers also lived in burghs. Scottish Kings encouraged the setting up of burghs in the hope that trade and crafts would flourish in them, making Scotland more prosperous. The King gave the important people in royal burghs (called 'BURGESSES') advantages over other merchants by giving them special privileges. These were written down in CHARTERS, like this charter of King David II (1364):

> *We have granted to our beloved Scottish burgesses freedom to buy and sell everywhere in their burghs. We forbid anyone to buy or sell wool, skins, hides, or other goods, except from the merchants of the burgh where they live. We order them to sell goods at the market place and cross of the burghs.*

Who controlled everyday life?

Most people in medieval Scotland were far from free to do as they wished. Ordinary farmers did not own the land they worked on, and they had to spend part of the year working for their landowner. They had to carry out duties. For example, the people who lived on land owned by the Abbey of Kelso had to:

> *pay six shillings and eight pence (33p) yearly and do these services: each man and his family to do four days harvest-time reaping, each to take one cartload of peats to the Abbey. Each of them to plough up $1\frac{1}{2}$ acres of the Abbey's land, to harrow for a day, find a man for rounding up sheep and another for shearing.*

◆ FEUDALISM – a system of duties, services, responsibilities and payments between different layers of society in western Europe during the Middle Ages

◆ OATH OF FEALTY – a promise made on the bible to be loyal to a king or lord

The people of Kelso, like most people in Western Europe at this time, were part of a system of duties, services, responsibilities and payments called FEUDALISM. Feudal society had several layers: people in each layer had duties to those above them and responsibilities to those below. Important men like earls and knights had duties such as fighting for the king: ordinary people performed more humble services – and expected to be protected in return. In each layer, too, someone receiving land had to swear an 'OATH OF FEALTY' like this one:

> *I swear on the Holy Gospel I shall be faithful to you my Lord against every man except the King. If I know you justly wish to go against anyone, I will help you. I will never do anything to harm or insult you.*

You notice that the oath was sworn on the Holy Gospel. All Scots were members of the Roman Catholic Church. In the medieval period most people in Western Europe were Roman Catholics, members of a Church led by the Pope. The Roman Catholic Church in Scotland struggled to remain free of the control of the English Archbishop of York. In 1192 the Pope agreed that the Catholic Church in Scotland was a separate organisation from the Catholic Church in England. Religion was very important in the lives of ordinary people. Sundays and Saints Days were special, and the local priest was an important man, able to read Latin in which the Bible was written.

There were church buildings all over Scotland. Throughout the countryside there were also castles – the strongholds of the knights, barons, earls, and other landowners. Originally these were built of wood, but by 1300 an increasing number were being replaced with stone castles.

Edinburgh Castle in 1300. This royal castle dominated Edinburgh from its position high above the burgh.

While their castles dominated the landscape, the landowners controlled the lives of the ordinary people who lived on their land. They held their own courts where they tried criminals, and even, at times, demanded that local men join their feudal armies.

STOP AND THINK

What sort of person would be best suited to rule over such a kingdom?

◆ Work in groups to note down the qualities you decide on.

How was Scotland governed?

On 14 October 1285 King Alexander III of Scotland married a young French noblewoman, Yolande of Dreux. The leaders of Scottish society rejoiced, because Alexander III's first wife, the sister of the English King Edward I, had died ten years earlier, and their two sons and daughter were also dead. (Although their daughter Margaret, Queen of Norway, had had a daughter of her own.) It was essential that the King have a healthy heir to avoid bitter quarrels about who should succeed him as ruler of Scotland. There was no elected government. The King was in charge and had a small royal household to help him run the country.

The royal household consisted of:

- The Constable – the chief military officer.
- The Marshall – in charge of the most expensive part of the army, the cavalry.
- The Chamberlain – in charge of finances from the royal lands and from burgh tolls and customs.
- The Steward – managed the royal household.
- The Chancellor – looked after the royal seal (that was stamped on documents) and the chapel: he was a record keeper and general administrator. Since he needed to be able to read and write, he was a churchman (a 'cleric') and he had other chaplains and clerics to help him in his work.

Besides his household officials, the King had to rely on his nobles to help him to rule. According to the feudal system, Scotland belonged to the King: he made grants of land to his great nobles, and in return they promised to control their local areas and to form feudal armies to help the King when he needed them.

In 1285 many nobles, along with their knights, were descendants of Frenchmen who had been part of the Norman Conquest of England and had married into English families. Scottish Kings brought in these Anglo-Normans to help them rule, granting them lands, as in this royal charter granting the head of the Bruce family:

> ***the land in Annandale, its woods, moors, streams, ponds and mills, with power there except in cases to be tried by the King.***

◆ JUSTICAR – a very senior official dealing with the law

◆ SHERIFF – a royal official responsible for a local area

Some nobles held royal positions. Three of them were JUSTICIARS who supervised the running of the country, travelling around it twice a year to hold courts. Twenty-six others held positions as SHERIFFS and managed local areas, usually from the security of a royal castle.

The Church looked to the King for protection: in 1285 its abbeys were prosperous communities with good farmland, helping the strength of the monarchy with the money they provided.

Jedburgh Abbey, one of several such buildings in the Borders, set amid rich farmland.

◆ OVERLORD – a king who was so important that other kings or princes accepted him as having rights over them and their lands

In 1285 Scots could look back over many years of peace and prosperity. Alexander III was on good terms with his brother-in-law, Edward I of England. In fact Alexander's ancestor, Malcolm III, had gained the Scottish crown with English help. Several Scottish rulers had spent time at the English court and there were marriages between people from the two countries. Several Scottish nobles also owned land in England. From time to time English Kings claimed to be the feudal OVERLORDS of Scottish Kings, but Alexander III had rejected this claim stating (according to the writings of a Dunfermline cleric in the early fourteenth century):

> ***Nobody but God himself has the right to take homage of my realm of Scotland.***

There seemed every reason, in 1285, for Scots to look forward to further times of peace and prosperity. But only five years after Alexander's marriage to Yolande of Dreux, Scotland's leading churchman, the Bishop of St. Andrews, wrote in despair to Edward I:

> ***There is fear of a general war and a large-scale slaughter unless God, through your active involvement and good offices, administer a quick cure.***

Why was there a crisis by the year 1290?

A timetable of the tragedy

18 March 1286 King Alexander set off from Edinburgh to join his new wife at Kinghorn. He rode on horseback on a stormy night, refusing to listen to those who told him not to travel. Three squires and two guides rode with him, but lost him in the darkness. The next day he was found dead, with his neck broken, on the shore; presumably he had fallen from his horse.

28 April 1286 The Scottish Parliament chose six leading men to be Guardians to rule the country. Guardians were needed because Alexander's only heir was Margaret, the three-year-old child of his daughter and her husband the King of Norway. The little girl was known as 'The Maid of Norway'.

6 November 1289 The **Treaty of Salisbury**: Scots, Norwegian, and English representatives agreed that Margaret should leave Norway and come to be Queen of Scotland.

18 July 1290 The **Treaty of Birgham**. It was agreed that Margaret would marry Edward I's son, Edward of Caernarfon, and that Scottish independence would be safeguarded. Scottish laws, liberties and customs were to be respected, its Parliament was only to meet in Scotland, its Church was to be free of outside interference, important positions were to be held by Scots and taxes raised in Scotland were just to be for Scottish needs.

28 August 1290 Edward I agreed to these terms at Northampton. Around this time, however, Edward took control of the Isle of Man which was part of the Scottish Kingdom. He also told the Scottish Guardians that he was appointing the Bishop of Durham to be his representative in Scotland to help run the country.

26 September 1290 On her journey from Norway, Margaret, Maid of Norway, died in Orkney. She was the last of the Canmore family who had ruled so well for over two centuries. Who would now be King?

Practise Your Skills

Answer the questions that follow, using the sources and your knowledge as appropriate.

Source A, from a promise made by the Scottish nobles to Alexander III, after his son's death in 1284:

'We faithfully promise that if our Lord King happens to die leaving no legitimate son or daughter of his body, or of Alexander his son, we will accept Margaret, daughter of our King's daughter Margaret, late Queen of Norway, as rightful heir of our King.'

1 Describe the reasons for this promise. (Demonstrate knowledge and understanding of historical developments, events and issues.)

Source B, from Edward I's promise in the Treaty of Birgham, 1290:

'The rights, laws, liberties and customs of Scotland in all matters and in all ways shall be wholly preserved for all time throughout the whole of that kingdom and its borders.'

2 How reliable is this account of Edward's intentions? (Evaluate historical sources and refer to their historical context.)

Source C, from the Bishop of St. Andrews' letter to Edward I, 1290 – the Bishop was one of the Guardians:

'There has been sounded through the people a sorrowful rumour that our Lady Margaret be dead, on which account the kingdom of Scotland is troubled. Robert Bruce has come with a great following to Perth, but what he intends to do we do not know. The Earls of Mar and Atholl are already collecting their army.'

3 Explain why this crisis had come about.
For question 3 you should write a short essay using Source C and your knowledge. You should include a brief introduction and conclusion. (Explain historical developments and events.)

Chapter 1: An overview

The People of Scotland …

- Mainly lived in the countryside: a small number lived in burghs.
- Had to work hard to survive.
- Had to carry out duties to their landowner.
- Had to promise to serve their landowner.

They had their lives shaped and controlled by …

The Church
The Roman Catholic Church was powerful, provided educated people, influenced lives in a religious age.

Nobles and Landowners
Controlled parts of Scotland from castles. Provided fighting men for the King.

Who in turn owed duties to …

The Monarch who …

Had to personally rule the country, make decisions, deal with enemies. Needed to trust his nobles.
But the monarchy was in trouble by 1290 because:

- Alexander III died in an accident in 1286.
- He left a three-year-old granddaughter, living in Norway to succeed him.
- She died when she was seven! So …
- A strong monarchy really mattered but it was not clear who would succeed to the crown. Confusion gave the English King, Edward I, the chance to interfere in Scottish affairs.

2 Edward I Takes Control

Key Points

This chapter looks at:

- The two main claimants to the Scottish crown.
- Why Edward I was able to decide who should rule Scotland, and how he used this power.
- His choice of John Balliol.
- Why Scots turned against Edward, fought him, but were defeated.

◆ GUARDIAN – a man chosen to rule the country because no adult King was available

Alexander III's death left Scotland in confusion. In 1290 Bishop Fraser of St. Andrews, one of the GUARDIANS OF SCOTLAND, wrote to Edward I of England asking for help to stop war breaking out between different men who wished to become the next King. The Bishop pleaded with Edward:

> ***By your active involvement and good offices, administer a quick cure.***

Other leading Scots agreed with the Bishop, and Edward needed little persuading. He was eager to take this chance to gain control of Scotland by making Scots accept him as their overlord.

In the year 1291 Edward and his advisers met leading Scots at Norham, on the English side of the River Tweed. His representative told the Scottish nobles:

> ***Our Lord King asks for your kind agreement and for recognition of his overlordship and he wishes to act with your advice in doing justice.***

Scottish nobles tried to avoid answering, saying that:

> ***They have no knowledge of your right, they have no power to reply to your claim without a Lord to whom the demand should be addressed.***

Edward then turned to the 'Competitors' who claimed the crown. With them he had more success. In June 1291 these Competitors agreed that he had the right to judge their claims and recognised him as their feudal superior in Scotland. In the Award of Norham they agreed that Edward:

> ***has shown us by good reasons that the sovereign lordship of the kingdom of Scotland and the right to try our claims belong to him. We, by our own free will, without any kind of constraint, do desire and grant that we should receive justice before him as Lord superior of the realm.***

Edward was now free to sit in judgement on the Competitors.

The competition for the crown

The Competitors

Thirteen people put forward claims – even the King of Norway tried his luck! But there were clearly really only two serious claimants. Both were from families that had once come over from Northern France as part of the Norman Conquest of England.

John Balliol might have said:

'My claim is the strongest of all – just look at the royal family tree. Now the descendants of King David's son William are dead, we must look to King David's other son (also David) for descendants to rule Scotland. His first child, Margaret, was my grandmother. I must be allowed the stronger claim. And I am related to the powerful Comyn family, which has helped rule Scotland for years. Bishop Fraser supports me too. I have lands in Northern France and England and have always been loyal to you, Lord Edward.'

Versus

Robert Bruce might have said:

'My claim is a very strong one. I may be approaching the age of 70, but look how closely I am related to the royal family of King David. King David's son David was my grandfather. I am a whole generation closer to the great King David than that troublemaker Balliol and his over-greedy Comyn relatives. King David knew what he was doing when he granted the lands of Annandale to our family. And you know, Lord Edward, that I am devoted to you and will serve you loyally.'

How was a decision made?

Balliol and Bruce were each asked to appoint 40 'auditors', men who would listen carefully to the arguments of each competitor and his lawyers. Edward I appointed another 24 auditors of his own. For nearly 16 months there was discussion, argument, and the gathering and presenting of evidence. It was not until 17 November 1292 that Edward I made his decision.

Everyone looked carefully at the Royal Family Tree

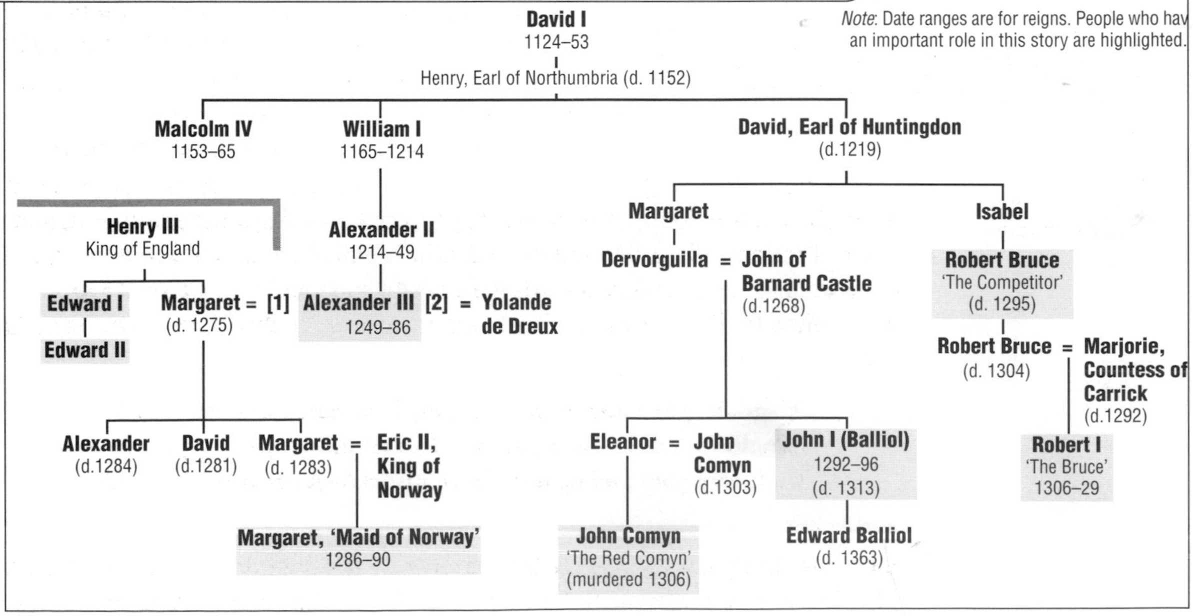

The Decision!

Edward chose Balliol. Nobody was very surprised at this decision. Many recognised that he had the stronger claim – even 29 of the auditors whom Bruce had chosen finally voted for Balliol. The Bruce family were angry, however. Bruce 'the Competitor' handed over his claims to his son (also Robert Bruce) who was the Earl of Carrick. The Earl had an 18-year-old son, who yet again was called Robert Bruce, and who was eager for his family to succeed. The Bruce family withdrew to their strongholds in the southwest. They were reluctant to recognise their new King and to do homage to him, and were determined to continue their claim.

The unhappy reign of King John, 1292–96

On St. Andrew's Day, 1292, Balliol was crowned on the Stone of Destiny at Scone Palace. On 26 December he was in Newcastle to swear to be loyal to his overlord, Edward I, by kneeling before him and declaring:

King John doing homage to Edward I.

I, John Balliol, King of Scots, hereby become your* LIEGEMAN *for the whole realm of Scotland and I will maintain faith and loyalty to you.

King John had the support of his relatives, the powerful Comyn family, which included the Earl of Buchan. He did not have the backing of the Bruce family and their friends, however. He extended royal power by setting up three new sheriffdoms in Skye, Lorne and Kintyre. But he achieved little else, because he soon found that his reign was dominated by Edward I's determination to exercise control over him.

At this time Edward not only faced Welsh opponents who resented his rule over them, but also the enmity of King Philip IV of France. Edward owned and ruled lands within France and the French King did not like the presence of another powerful ruler in France. Edward was determined that he would at least keep a tight grip over Scotland.

◆ LIEGEMAN – subject of a feudal superior

The result for King John was misery and humiliation. Offenders punished in Scottish courts found that they could appeal to Edward against Scottish legal decisions. Though only a few did so, Edward handled these appeals in a way that brought shame on the Scottish King. In 1293 he forced John to attend a meeting of the English Parliament in London to argue his case. A chronicler, a few years later wrote:

Standing in court in front of him, John carried out Edward's orders and having experienced many insults from all, contrary to his kingly rank and dignity, he returned home greatly crestfallen.

John was clearly not going to be treated as Scots felt their King should be treated. In 1294 Edward went even further in trying to control the Scottish King. He demanded that John, ten of his earls and sixteen of his barons, with their fighting men, should join him on his campaign against the French. This was too much for the Scottish nobles who were afraid that John might give way to Edward again. In 1295, led by the Comyns, the nobles took most of the King's power from him. They set up a council of twelve bishops, earls and barons to govern the country.

STOP AND THINK

Could King John have acted differently?

- Work with a partner: one of you lists every reason why King John could not have acted differently than he did, the other argues that a different course of action was possible.

Edward's revenge

Far from helping Edward, the Scottish nobles opened up discussions with Philip IV, which led to an alliance between Scotland and France in October 1295. Each side promised to help the other if attacked by the King of England: the French by trying to keep English forces busy well away from Scotland, and the Scots by directly attacking England. Scottish leaders rejected Edward's claim to be their overlord and sent a letter in their King's name, noting on his behalf that Edward had:

> ***caused harm to the liberties of ourselves and our kingdom by summoning us outside our realm at the mere beck and call of anybody.***

In 1296 Edward, now 58 years old, gathered a large army and marched north, sending his fleet with supplies up the eastern coast. For their part the Scottish leaders called their feudal army to gather near Selkirk on 11 March 1296. The Comyns led this resistance to Edward I. The Bruces stayed loyal to Edward. In the west, the Scots invaded England. An English chronicler of the time wrote:

> ***Sir John Comyn invaded England with an army of Scots, burning houses, slaughtering men and driving off cattle and on the two days following they attacked Carlisle. But failing in their attempt, they withdrew.***

Carlisle was too strong to capture. Its castle was commanded by Robert Bruce (the Competitor's son, now Lord of Annandale after his father's death). Scottish forces did as much damage as they could in brutal raids on the North of England. While they did so Edward brought his experienced army of around 25,000 infantry, plus 4,000 cavalry, up the east coast to Berwick on Tweed, Scotland's chief port and wool trade centre. The town refused to surrender but was easily captured. It was then subjected to a three-day fury of destruction and killing, aimed at terrifying the Scots.

The English army moved steadily north. At Dunbar the Scottish army abandoned a strong position to attack the English forces led by Edward's senior commander, John de Warrene, Earl of Surrey. The attack was easily stopped, and many of the Scots were killed or captured as they fled, trying to reach the safety of a nearby forest. No other force remained to block Edward. He marched steadily north, taking control of key castles as he did so. At Stirling a chronicler of the time noted:

> ***... they that were in the castle ran away and left none but the porter who did hand over the keys.***

Edward went as far as Elgin before returning into England, stopping at burghs, abbeys and castles so that local leaders could swear loyalty to him. On 2 July 1296, King John was forced to surrender his kingdom. He was sent first to the Tower of London, then to Hertford, where he was allowed to keep a huntsman and ten hounds. In response to a request from the Pope he was sent to France in 1299, and in 1301 was released altogether to live on his French lands. But Scots who hoped he might return were disappointed, as John died in 1313 without leaving France.

◆ GOVERNOR – The English King's representative in Scotland, controlling the country for his master

◆ TREASURER – in charge of Scottish money matters for Edward I

The Bruce family suggested that perhaps Robert Bruce might now occupy the vacant throne. Edward dismissed their claim. Although he could not absorb Scotland into his kingdom, as he had done with the principality of Wales, he installed his men in positions of power. The Earl of Surrey (John Balliol's father-in-law) became his GOVERNOR and Hugh Cressingham took control of finances as TREASURER. There were other English officials in lesser posts, such as the Sheriff of Lanark.

Scottish leaders hurried to make peace with Edward, signing and sealing an oath of loyalty on a document now known as the Ragman Roll. Among the 1,500 signatures were those of Robert Bruce, Lord of Annandale, and his son Robert (now Earl of Carrick). As a final show of his power, Edward had the Stone of Destiny and other important Scottish objects carried off to London.

Practise Your Skills

Answer the questions that follow, using the sources and your knowledge as appropriate.

Source A, from an English chronicler's description of the siege and capture of Berwick by Edward I (1296):

'The King tried to persuade the leading men to surrender, promising them personal safety, security for their possessions, pardon for their offences. He waited for three days. They gave no reply to his generous offer. He spoke to them in a friendly manner; they redoubled their insults. Some of them putting themselves on the heights, bared their buttocks and insulted the King. Others fiercely attacked the fleet. Troops were brought into action and the city occupied. No fewer than fifteen thousand men and women perished, some by the sword, others by fire.'

1 Does Source A provide an accurate account of the siege and destruction of Berwick? (Evaluate historical sources with reference to their context.)

Source B, from a letter sent by King John to Edward I, April 1296:

'... you and others of your kingdom have committed repeatedly and by violent force intolerable injuries and severe damages against us and our kingdom and have come with a vast crowd of soldiers and committed acts of slaughter and burning. We cannot any longer endure these insults and we renounce the fealty and homage which we have done to you.'

Source C, from a letter from King John to Edward I, July 1296:

'Through bad advice and our own foolishness we have angered our lord Edward in that while we still owed him fealty and homage we made an alliance with the King of France against him, we have defied him, renouncing our homage, we have sent men into England to burn and murder. For these many wrongs our lord the King of England has conquered Scotland, something he had a right to do.'

2 In what ways, and for what reasons, do Sources B and C differ from one another? (Evaluate sources – making a comparison between sources.)

Chapter 2: An overview

The intervention of Edward I

- Leading Scots asked him to help choose their next King.
- Edward made those wanting the crown accept him as overlord.
- Everyone's claim was carefully studied.

The two main Competitors

John Balliol
Balliol claimed that he was the person most directly descended from the royal family.

Versus

Robert Bruce
Bruce claimed he was also descended from the royal family but was a whole generation closer to it than Balliol.

- Both families had powerful friends and relatives in Scotland.
- Both families also had lands in England.
- Both Competitors promised loyalty to Edward.

Edward chose John

Bruce went off, angry.

King John's unhappy reign

- Edward treated John badly, and ordered him about.
- Edward demanded Scottish help in his war with France.
- Scottish leaders refused, broke away from Edward, and signed a treaty with France.
- Scots, led by the Comyns, attacked the North of England.
- Edward's army destroyed Scottish army at Dunbar. Edward took John away.
- Englishmen became key officials in Scotland.

3 William Wallace's Astonishing Life

Key Points

This chapter looks at:

- Wallace's importance, yet the limited amount of reliable evidence about him.
- Wallace's rising against English rule.
- His victory in the Battle of Stirling Bridge.
- His time as Guardian of Scotland.
- His downfall and execution.

Portrait of Wallace, painted in 1633 by Sir George Jamesone.

William Wallace – a mysterious man?

In May 1297 a group of Scots led by William Wallace killed the Sheriff of Lanark, William Heselrig, one of Edward I's officials in Scotland. This attack shocked the other English officials in Scotland, and Wallace became a man they were eager to catch. But who was he?

Look at the portrait on the left. Is this what Wallace looked like? But notice it was produced long after his life. Perhaps written descriptions will help. This was written by a Scottish chronicler of long ago:

Wallace [had] the body of a giant, cheerful in appearance with agreeable features, broad-shouldered and big-boned. A most spirited fighting man.

But Walter Bower wrote this around the year 1440 – more than a century after Wallace's death. Bower therefore can never have seen Wallace. So, it seems that finding first-hand evidence about Wallace is not easy. The historian Geoffrey Barrow notes in *Robert the Bruce* (1988): 'We know less about Wallace than we know about almost any of the great national figures of our history.' And the historian Andrew Fisher writes in *William Wallace* (1986): 'Wallace is at best a shadowy figure and likely to remain so.'

The difficulties with evidence about Wallace

There are several problems in finding reliable historical evidence that gives us information about Wallace's life and activities.

- The historian Edward Cowan explains in *Images of Scotland* (1997):

  Strictly contemporary materials for the career of Wallace are distressingly scanty. Only three documents from Wallace himself survive – a charter, a safe conduct for three monks, and a letter to the town of Lubeck. The earliest Scottish narrative was compiled around the year 1370.

- We have neither a drawing or painting of Wallace, nor a written description, from people who actually met him. We cannot be sure when he was born, and there is even a dispute about whether he was born at Elderslie in Renfrewshire or Ellerslie in Ayrshire.
- Chroniclers who wrote about him much nearer to his lifetime were English, and so were very unsympathetic to him.
- Of course Scottish chroniclers who wrote about him between 1370 and 1480 may have been using all sorts of evidence from Wallace's time which has since disappeared. But as we cannot be absolutely sure about this, we cannot completely rely on their evidence.
- These Scottish chroniclers were strong supporters of Scottish independence and the Scottish monarchy. They chose to mention whatever fitted these beliefs and we cannot tell what they left out because it did not fit their beliefs. The most famous chronicler is known as 'Blind Harry'. He wrote his account in 1478, in part at least, to help those who thought that the King at the time (James III) was far too sympathetic to the English. The colourful story of Wallace helped to stir anti-English feeling.

STOP AND THINK

Why is it such a problem for us to fully understand William Wallace?

Wallace bursts on to the scene

The death of the Sheriff Heselrig was an important event. So, who was Wallace, the man who had killed him? He was the second son of a knight whose lands lay in areas dominated by the power of a leading nobleman, James Stewart.

What Wallace did was not unique. At the time of Heselrig's murder, English control of Scotland was already slipping away. In the area of the Black Isle and Moray, Andrew Murray, a nobleman's son, led Scottish forces to capture English strongholds in Inverness, Elgin and Banff. There was anti-English activity in Aberdeenshire and the West Highlands. In the southwest the young Robert Bruce, Earl of Carrick, joined the movement in which James Stewart and Robert Wishart, Bishop of Glasgow, were also active. So why did Wallace become so important? He brought a fierce energy to the war. He continued to kill other English officials and burned buildings. About 70 years after these events a Scottish chronicler noted how Wallace's fame had grown:

> ***From that time all those people who hated the English flocked to him and he became their leader. He was wondrously brave and bold.***

Who made up a thirteenth-century army?

An early fourteenth-century illustration of soldiers fighting with the weapons of the time. Their clothes do not give them much protection.

The knights

Knights were the cavalry soldiers. They were wealthy men able to afford costly (and heavy) metal armour and the powerful horses needed to carry them. At this time most armour was made of small linked iron-rings called 'mail'. The horses needed lots of food: this meant that campaigns usually only took place in summer. Knights fought using lances, swords, axes and maces. A large number of cavalry, charging at the enemy, formed a terrifying and powerful force which was hard to stop. But they were only effective on firm ground – horses could not move so quickly on soft ground. English armies were wealthier than Scottish armies and so usually had far more knights.

The infantry

Wallace is said to have liked to fight on foot using a five-foot-long two-handed sword. Ordinary soldiers fought on foot using spears, swords, and daggers. Scottish armies were specially fond of using spears which were often ten to twelve feet long. Well-organised spearmen packed in close ranks were difficult to attack and could beat off cavalry. But they were not well protected from an attack by archers. Many could not afford costly armour. They often wore metal helmets but the rest of their clothing was usually made of heavily padded woollen cloth, or leather. Once close to the enemy their fighting became a mass of jabbing, stabbing and slashing in a noisy and terrifying confusion.

The archers

Longbowmen

English armies used longbowmen, many of them Welsh. They were able to fire metal-tipped arrows considerable distances, accurately, rapidly, and with enough force to pierce mail. Scottish armies did not have many bowmen. Longbowmen needed both strength and skill. They also needed protection from enemy cavalry. Much practice was needed to be a skilled archer. Getting a big enough supply of arrows was also a problem, because they could fire so many in a short time.

Crossbowmen

The crossbow was even more accurate and deadly than the longbow but it took a long time to load. A crossbowman could only fire one arrow to a longbowman's three or four. Neither English nor Scottish soldiers used this weapon, but English leaders sometimes hired crossbowmen from the continent where it was much more popular. Crossbowmen got higher pay than other soldiers.

Among those who joined Wallace was a knight famous for his violence, Sir William Douglas. Together they launched a daring raid on Scone, the ancient centre for the crowning of Scottish Kings and the base of William Ormsby, the English justiciar who controlled the area. Ormsby managed to escape, but left behind all his valuable possessions which were triumphantly seized by Wallace.

While Wallace carried out his raids, Scottish nobles led by James Stewart gathered an army. English chroniclers criticised their behaviour, writing that:

> ***Hardly had six months passed since the Scots had bound themselves by a solemn oath to the King of the English when the reviving malice of that race excited their minds to rebellion. The Bishop of Glasgow, ever foremost in treason, plotted with the Steward of the realm named James for a new chapter of ruin.***

The chronicler even blamed the nobles for stirring Wallace to action. A formidable English army raised in the north and led by Robert Clifford and Henry Percy

Wallace victorious – the Battle of Stirling Bridge, 11 September 129

Battle of Stirling Bridge
by William Hole (1846–1917).

1 The Scots

Wallace and Murray had joined forces. They could not rely on the Scottish nobles providing them with cavalry and planned to fight on foot. They placed their army on the slopes of Abbey Craig about a mile from the narrow bridge over the Forth that made this place so important to control.

2 The English

The Earl of Surrey and Hugh Cressingham led a far bigger army than Wallace and Murray. They had archers and plenty of cavalry and were very confident. They camped outside the burgh of Stirling across the river from the Scots.

3 Delay

Although as many as 5,000 English troops crossed the bridge in the early morning, they were recalled because Surrey had overslept. There were more delays while he knighted several soldiers, and had discussions with two Scottish nobles, James Stewart and the Earl of Lennox. These men had promised they would try and persuade Wallace and Murray to make peace. Surrey sent two friars to ask the Scots to negotiate peace. All these efforts failed.

advanced into Scotland and faced the Scottish army at Irvine. After long negotiations, the Scots surrendered. Murray and Wallace were, however, still very active, and were joined by others including MacDuff, son of the Earl of Fife. Control of more and more of the country slipped away from English officials. In July Hugh Cressingham wrote in despair to his master Edward I:

> ***By far the greater part of your counties in the Scottish kingdom are still not provided with officials, they have been killed, besieged or imprisoned or have abandoned their positions and dare not go back. In some shires the Scots have appointed and established officials. No shire is properly ruled save for Berwickshire and Roxburghshire and they only recently.***

With Edward busy with his French war it was left to the Earl of Surrey, as governor of Scotland, and Hugh Cressingham to gather a huge army to crush Scottish resistance, especially that of Wallace.

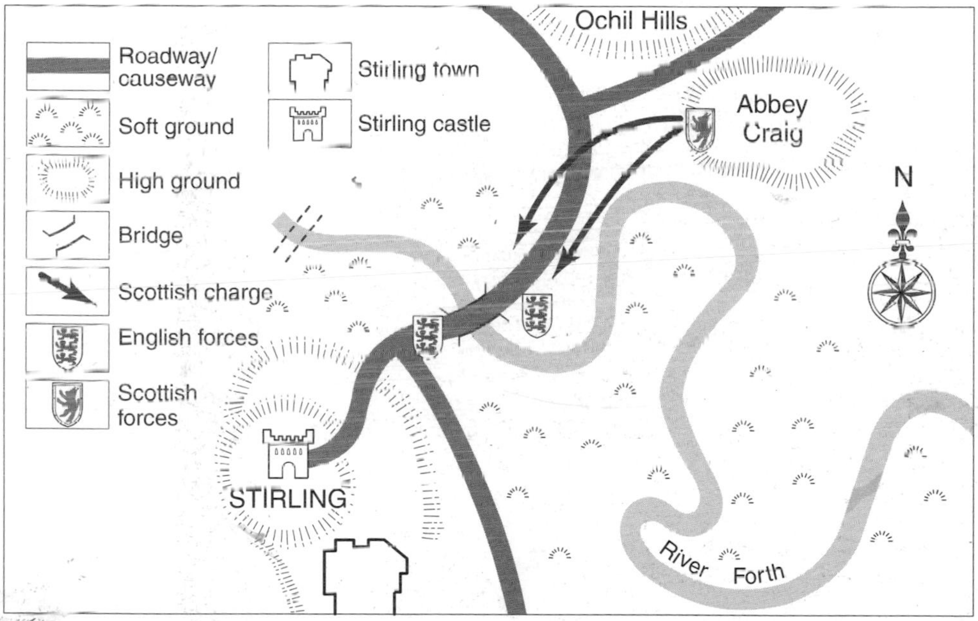

4 Attack!

The narrow wooden bridge, the soft ground and the small space to fight in, caused by bends in the river, worried Sir Richard Lundie, a Scottish knight fighting with Surrey. However, his plan to go to a ford upstream with a force of 600 and attack from the side was rejected. Cressingham led the English forces as they again crossed the bridge.

5 Defeat

When around 5,000 English soldiers had crossed the bridge, the Scots attacked. The English knights could not manoeuvre and the English were driven back, killed, wounded and drowned in the river. The wooden bridge collapsed. Surrey and the rest of the army watched the slaughter from the other side of the river, powerless to intervene.

6 Victory

The remainder of the English army fled. Stewart and Lennox, who had watched the battle, now attacked the English with their cavalry. In the battle and the retreat several thousand English soldiers and one hundred English knights died. One of them was Cressingham. The Scots hated him so much that they flayed his skin from his body, cut it into strips and used it for sword belts and other items.

Wallace – Guardian of Scotland, 1298

Stirling Bridge was a remarkable victory for foot-soldiers. After the battle, the English-held castles at Stirling and Dundee surrendered, providing further success for the Scottish forces led by Wallace and Murray. Although Wallace and Murray were not the heads of great noble families, their military success meant that the nobles chose them as Guardians of Scotland. A few weeks later, in November, Murray died, leaving Wallace as sole Guardian.

Wallace's status was raised when one of the earls knighted him. His aim was not power for himself, but to restore King John as ruler of an independent Scotland. The little evidence that has survived shows that Wallace described himself as:

> *William Wallace, Knight, Guardian of the King of Scotland and commander of its army in the name of the famous prince Lord John, by God's grace illustrious King of Scotland, by consent of the community of the realm.*

However, some Scottish chroniclers, and some historians, suggest that great nobles were not enthusiastic about giving their consent, because Wallace was not their social equal.

The only English garrisons remaining were those in Edinburgh and Roxburgh so Wallace was free to take his men on a savage raid of the North of England. There they did great damage, killing, burning and looting. An English chronicler wrote at the time:

> *William Wallace is the leader of these savages; these wicked men delivered Alnwick to the flames. Now the wicked people return to Scotland and the honour of a knighthood is given to Wallace. From a robber he became a knight just as a swan is made out of a raven.*

Wallace announced his success against the English in letters to Northern European ports, such as this one to Lubeck in Germany (October 1297), urging them to trade with Scotland and to:

> *Tell your merchants that they can have safe access to all the ports of Scotland because the kingdom of Scotland has been recovered from the power of the English.*

Wallace also used peaceful methods to promote the Scottish cause. The Catholic Church was so important that it was vital for Wallace to have the support of the clergy. Wallace made sure that, when a new Bishop of St. Andrews was needed, the man appointed, William Lamberton, was loyal to the cause of Scottish independence. When Lamberton was in Rome to be consecrated by Pope Boniface in June 1298, he helped persuade the Pope to support the cause. But peaceful times in Scotland were all too brief. In 1298 Edward I returned from his French wars, gathered an army and began advancing north.

Wallace's downfall – the Battle of Falkirk, 22 July 1298

The English army of around 14,000 men was far larger than the Scottish army, and included far more archers and knights, and even had crossbowmen from Normandy. The Scottish army retreated north. Edward had to follow although it was a struggle to feed his forces in areas that the Scottish army had stripped of food. Edward had further problems as quarrels began between his Welsh and English soldiers. Edward was relieved when two Scottish nobles loyal to him, Earl Patrick of Dunbar and the Earl of Angus, told him that the Scots were nearby. It meant that by making a rapid march, Edward could force the Scots into battle against him when they may not have wanted to fight.

Wallace's army stood with woodland behind them and a burn in front. He arranged his foot-soldiers in four great circles. With the soldiers standing and kneeling in rows and their spears pointing outwards the circles would be difficult for calvary to attack. These formations, called 'shiltrons', needed protection from arrows and for this Wallace relied on the Comyns and other earls with their cavalry unit of 500. A small number of Scottish archers were also present, standing separately between the shiltrons.

The English knights charged, their terrifying power causing the Scottish knights to flee without a fight. This left the Scottish archers exposed and they were killed. But the shiltrons held. Edward sent his longbowmen and crossbowmen forward, knowing there were now no Scottish cavalrymen to ride the archers down. The Scots had to stand while arrows poured into them, killing and wounding so many that great gaps were left in the shiltrons into which the English knights charged. Wallace retreated. On the battlefield, an English chronicler of the time wrote that the Scottish soldiers:

> ***fell like blossoms in an orchard when the fruit has ripened. Their bodies covered the ground as thickly as snow in winter.***

Some Scottish chroniclers claimed that Robert Bruce, Earl of Carrick, helped Edward I: historians now think he was not involved in any way. Wallace's rise had been due to his military skill and success, so after this defeat he resigned as Guardian. Having secured victory in Scotland, Edward returned to his campaign in France.

The last years, 1298–1305

John Comyn and Robert Bruce, Earl of Carrick, replaced Wallace as joint Guardians. Wallace travelled to the continent to join in the effort to win the Pope's support, and to free John Balliol. This effort met with some success. In 1299, Pope Boniface put out a statement to Edward I declaring:

> ***The realm of Scotland belongs to the Roman Church and it was not and is not lawful for you to dominate it by force.***

Edward I was persuaded to release Balliol to the Pope. By 1301 Balliol was free and living in his French lands. But Scots like Wallace who hoped that he would return to rule Scotland were disappointed. Guardians continued to manage the country (as much as English forces allowed them).

The joint Guardianship was not a happy experiment – Comyn and Bruce were bitter rivals. Quarrels and at least one fight flared up between them, till in 1300 Bruce resigned his position. Yet Scottish leadership needed to be strong because when in 1300 Edward I returned again from his French campaigns, he began to try to secure control over Scotland. Robert Bruce submitted to Edward I in 1302. Edward's position was greatly helped in 1303 when the French King's need for peace forced him to abandon his Scottish allies and sign a peace treaty with Edward.

In 1303 and 1304 Edward's military pressure was so strong that Comyn and the Scottish leaders were ready to make peace and recognise Edward as their overlord. Edward was careful not to be too harsh with these men. Even William Oliphant, who defended Stirling Castle for three months till July 1304, escaped execution and was only imprisoned for four years. He later fought for his English overlord, Edward II.

But for Wallace there was to be no forgiveness. When he returned from the continent Wallace became actively involved in the resistance campaign of 1300–04. In 1304, he refused to submit when all around were doing so. The Scottish Parliament that met in St. Andrews to confirm the peace with Edward declared Wallace an outlaw. Edward encouraged Wallace's former allies to hunt him down. The Scottish chronicler Walter Bower, writing in the 1440s, noted:

> ***The noble William was afraid of the treachery of his countrymen. Some of them envied him for his uprightness, others were won over by promises, others prepared traps for him, hoping thereby for the favour of the King of England.***

On 3 August 1305 Wallace was finally caught. His captor was the Scottish knight Sir John Mentieth who had fought against Edward till 1304, and was later to help Robert Bruce. But now he handed Wallace over to English soldiers and was rewarded with the post of Sheriff of Dumbarton. Wallace was taken to London and led through jeering crowds to Westminster Hall. There on 23 August he was denounced as a traitor and an outlaw, and pronounced guilty. Outlaws were denied proper trials so no witnesses were called, and Wallace was not allowed to defend himself. He was then subjected to the dreadful punishment of hanging, drawing and quartering, given to people declared to be both traitors and outlaws. The terrible cruelty of this form of execution was meant to frighten others who might think of opposing the King.

Wallace was dragged on a wooden frame to Smithfield outside London. There he was hanged, but he was cut down before he died to have his intestines hacked out (drawn) and burned. He was beheaded and his head stuck on a pole at Westminster Bridge. The rest of his body was cut in quarters, and parts were sent to Newcastle, Berwick, Perth and Stirling. His career as a leader of the fight for Scottish independence had lasted just eight years.

Practise Your Skills

Answer the questions that follow, using the sources and your knowledge as appropriate.

Source A, from the writings of an English chronicler Walter of Guisborough in about 1297:

'A public robber called William Wallace, a vagrant fugitive, called all the exiles to himself and made himself almost their prince. They grew to be numerous.'

1 Discuss the value of Source A to someone studying these times. (Evaluate sources with reference to their historical context.)

Source B, from an English chronicler of the time about the Battle of Stirling Bridge:

'Thus all these experienced men, though they knew the enemy was at hand, began to pass over a bridge so narrow that even two horsemen could scarcely ride side by side. So they did all morning until the vanguard was on one side of the river and the remainder of the army on the other.'

2 Describe the main events of the Battle of Stirling Bridge. (Demonstrate knowledge and understanding of historical development, events and issues.)

Source C, from the writings of the Scottish chronicler John of Fordun in 1270:

'In the year 1305 William Wallace was craftily captured by a Scotsman, John of Mentieth, who handed him over to the English and in London he was torn limb from limb and, as a warning to the Scots, his limbs were hung on towers throughout England and Scotland.'

3 Explain why Wallace was so cruelly treated. (Explain historical development and events.)

Chapter 3: An overview

Wallace's rising, 1297

- Wallace killed an English sheriff.
- He raided Scone. His efforts attracted men to him.
- Andrew Murray and others also attacked English forces.

Wallace's military success

- Scots nobles gave in to the English at Irvine.
- Wallace and Murray faced a huge English army at Stirling Bridge.
- By skilfully making the most of their strengths and English mistakes, they won a great victory.

Wallace as Guardian

- Wallace attacked the North of England.
- He appointed a bishop and encouraged trade.
- Edward I's victory at Falkirk ended Wallace's success.

Wallace's downfall, 1305

- Wallace visited the continent.
- He fought in the campaign 1300–4.
- He refused to submit and was captured.
- He was tried and executed.

4 Robert Bruce and Resistance

Key Points

This chapter looks at:

- How Robert Bruce first became King.
- The opposition to him of some Scots and of English forces.
- His initial defeat and gradual recovery.
- His triumph at the Battle of Bannockburn.

Robert Bruce with his first wife, Isobel of Mar. This portrait was produced in 1591.

A killing ... and a crown

In 1304 Edward I left Scotland for the last time. With the advice of three Scottish leaders, including Robert Bruce, he set up a new system of government. Englishmen held the most important posts, but Scottish nobles were also part of it. John Balliol clearly did not wish to return and his young son, Edward, was in King Edward's hands.

Bruce had supported Edward since the winter of 1301–02. He served as Sheriff of Lanark and Ayr. He was present at the siege of Stirling. In 1304, his first wife having died, he married Elizabeth, daughter of Edward I's ally, the Earl of Ulster.

But Bruce still had ambitions. By now his father had died and he was not only Earl of Carrick but Lord of Annandale too. Bruce had made peace with Edward when John Balliol's cause seemed to be reviving. But now that cause had been defeated. Moreover, as Edward I was 67, he was not likely to live much longer. Bruce began discussions to support his own claim for the crown.

His first meeting went well. He won the friendship of William Lamberton, Bishop of St. Andrews. The next meeting was to be much more difficult because it was with John Comyn, leader of Scotland's most powerful family and John Balliol's nephew. The two men had been on bad terms for some time, and it seemed sensible to meet in as safe a place as possible – a church, where fighting was forbidden. On 10 February 1306, they came together before the high altar of Greyfriars Church in Dumfries.

We do not know what discussions were held, but violence broke out and John Comyn was wounded. Further confusion followed, which ended with Bruce's supporters (his brother-in-law, Christopher Seton, and James Kirkpatrick), killing John Comyn and Comyn's uncle Robert.

A violent death in a church was a terrible event. The Church at this time was very powerful and did not like its rules being broken. Moreover, the Comyn family would no doubt want revenge. Bruce faced ruin, being EXCOMMUNICATED and hunted as an outlaw. He had to act quickly.

◆ EXCOMMUNICATION – being cast out of the Roman Catholic Church

Church support was vital. When the Pope eventually heard what had happened he did excommunicate Bruce, but by then, leaders of the Scottish Church led by Robert Wishart, Bishop of Glasgow, and the Bishops of St. Andrews and Moray were supporting him. All three totally opposed Edward I and were afraid that the Scottish Church would fall under English control.

Next Bruce secured control over castles in southwest Scotland. Then he travelled to the ancient centre of Scottish kingship, Scone. On 25 March 1306 he was proclaimed King. His four brothers, the three bishops and two leading abbots, the Earls of Atholl, Lennox and Mentieth and several lesser nobles such as James Douglas, all gathered around him. By tradition the Earl of Fife should have carried out the ceremony, but he was not available. Instead his sister, Isabel, even though she was married to the Comyn Earl of Buchan, hurried to Scone. On 27 March, in a second ceremony in Scone Abbey she placed a simple crown, a circle of gold, on Robert Bruce's head.

English garrisons held the main strongholds in Scotland. The Comyn family and their allies, such as the MacDougalls of Argyll, were eager for revenge. Many Scots were shocked by what had happened. Edward did not hear the news for two weeks. Then he made Aymer de Valence his commander in Scotland and issued orders:

> *All those who were present at the death of Sir John Comyn [are to] be drawn and hanged. And all those who agreed to it, and those who afterwards received them willingly, knowing the deed was done, to have the same judgement. And those who are or will be captured bearing arms against the King be hanged or beheaded.*

The modern historian Fiona Watson described the situation (*Image and Identity*, 1998):

> A very large section of the Scottish political community (and many of their followers) perceived that their duty was to fight against him [Bruce] ... for a number of years after 1306, most Scots preferred to live under an English King rather than accept a murderous Scottish usurper.

A downward slide to defeat, 1306–07

Bruce's forces attacked various places held by their Scottish enemies, but soon had to stop to face two English armies. One attacked the southwest. The main army, led by Aymer de Valence, moved into central Scotland. It was supported by many Scots, especially the Comyns and the MacDougalls of Argyll. Bishops Wishart and Lamberton were captured and put in prison in England. The Bishop of Moray fled first to Orkney, then to Norway. Bruce gathered a small army and advanced on de Valence's forces, which were based in Perth, and offered to fight. De Valence refused. Bruce's army retreated to Methven.

Edward I wrote to the Pope:

> *The Bishop of Moray by preaching so much against [me] and urging his flock to rebel with Sir Robert Bruce has stirred them up.*

On 19 June 1306 de Valence's army took Bruce's force by surprise, destroyed most of it and captured many of its leaders. Bruce managed to escape. The remainder of his army fled west and were overwhelmed by a force of MacDougalls at Dalry. Bruce no longer had an army. He had sent his wife, sister and daughter to be safe in Kildrummy Castle where his brother Neil was in charge. De Valence took the castle. Neil Bruce was captured, hanged and beheaded. The Earl of Atholl escaped with Bruce's female relatives.

The English chronicle of Lanercost described Edward's army in Scotland:

> *They took all the castles. They hanged those that took part in the conspiracy, most of whom they caused first to be drawn at the heels of horses. Among them was the Englishman Christopher Seton who had married Bruce's sister. They also took to England the Bishop of St. Andrews, also the Bishop of Glasgow and the Abbot of Scone who had assisted Robert Bruce.*

At Tain, Atholl and his group were captured by the Earl of Ross and handed over to Edward I. Bruce's wife was put in prison and his daughter in a nunnery in Yorkshire. His sister Mary was imprisoned in a cage at Roxburgh Castle. The same punishment was given to Isabel, Countess of Buchan, locked in a cage hung outside Berwick Castle walls. Both were released in 1310. Bruce fled to Kintyre and from there had to leave the mainland altogether.

Bruce's recovery, 1307–14

In February 1307 Robert Bruce and a small group of followers landed near Turnberry. His brothers Thomas and Alexander landed with a small force in Galloway which was promptly attacked and defeated by Dungal MacDougall and local clansmen. Bruce hid in the hills. His brothers were taken away and executed. Yet seven years after this dark time, he had won control over almost all of the mainland.

STOP AND THINK

What might have made it possible for Bruce to recover from this desperate situation?

- Note down your thoughts. Read on and compare your ideas with what happened.

Did Bruce succeed because he was enormously popular?

The historian Fiona Watson suggests (in *Image and Identity*):

> The fact that Bruce succeeded (and it was touch and go for many months) attests more to his tenacity, ruthlessness and ability than the willingness of the Scottish nation to follow him. He became King in more than name only when he had conquered Scotland from other Scots.

Bruce had powerful enemies among the Scottish nobles. Indeed some were so much against him that they left Scotland when Bruce triumphed, and are known as 'the Disinherited'. They hoped that King John's son, Edward Balliol, would return.

Did Bruce succeed because of a change of English King?

On 7 July 1307 that outstanding old soldier Edward I died. His son now became King Edward II, and found that his father's costly wars had left England with a huge debt. Edward II was not an able soldier nor a strong leader. He ended his father's big campaign in Scotland, but soon found several of his powerful English nobles opposing him at home. They especially hated the King's favourite, the French Knight Piers Gaveston. Edward soon had so many problems to deal with at home that he could not turn his attention to Scotland for three years.

Did Bruce succeed because he was a fine soldier?

Bruce had learned to fight in conditions that suited him. He developed an army that could move quickly. He used the countryside very skilfully. He launched sudden surprise attacks, then vanished. At the Battle of Loudon Hill (10 May 1307), for example, he defeated de Valence's larger cavalry force by picking a battleground that did not suit the English knights. Much of the land was mossy. Bruce had ditches dug to make it even more difficult for horsemen, causing them to fight in a very small space. A Scot with de Valence's army wrote:

> *The people believe that Bruce will carry all before him, encouraged by false preachers from Bruce's army.*

Bruce took castle after castle with sudden fierce attacks, often in the dark, scaling battlements with rope ladders, and destroying the castles he captured. In January 1313 he took the strongly-defended key centre of Perth from a garrison led by Sir William Oliphant (who had once held Stirling Castle against Edward I). His many Scottish opponents were far too widely scattered to fight together: Bruce was able to defeat them one by one. He had capable supporters such as Sir James Douglas. Even the Comyn family were overcome. On 23 May 1308 Bruce's experienced soldiers defeated the Earl of Buchan's men: the Earl fled to England. After this battle Bruce ruthlessly destroyed the Comyn power-base in the northeast. The MacDougalls were defeated too, trapped in the Pass of Brander between Bruce's men and Highlanders led by James Douglas.

Did Bruce succeed because he was a good political leader?

Bruce was fierce with long-standing enemies. But others like the Earl of Ross, Thomas Randolph, the Earl of Atholl and Sir John Mentieth were won over to his side. The Bishop of Moray returned. In March 1309 he called a meeting of the Scottish Parliament, which declared that he was the lawful King. In 1310 the Scottish Church leaders declared support for Bruce.

By the summer of 1314 only Berwick, Bothwell and Stirling Castle were in English hands. Scottish resistance to Bruce had been broken. Edward II had to act, not only to recover control of Scotland, but also to stop the raids on the North of England that Bruce had begun in 1311. The historian R. C. Paterson notes (in *For the Lion*, 1996) that: 'The situation in the Northern Counties became so bad that normal life could only continue by permission of the Scots.'

Edward's immediate aim was to free Stirling Castle, defended by a Scot, Sir Philip Mowbray, from Bruce's forces. Mowbray and Edward Bruce agreed that if the castle were not relieved by midsummer, the English would surrender it.

The Battle of Bannockburn 23–24 June 1314

Edward II's army was large and had many knights. Several of Bruce's leading Scottish enemies, like the Earl of Angus and John Comyn's son, came too. But Bruce's smaller force was now very experienced and had time to prepare for battle. Bruce chose his battlefield carefully and made it even more difficult for English forces in ways described by a chronicler:

> *The Scots dug extended ditches three feet deep and three feet wide from the right to the left of the army, filling them with twigs, reeds and sticks and covering them with grass and weeds.*

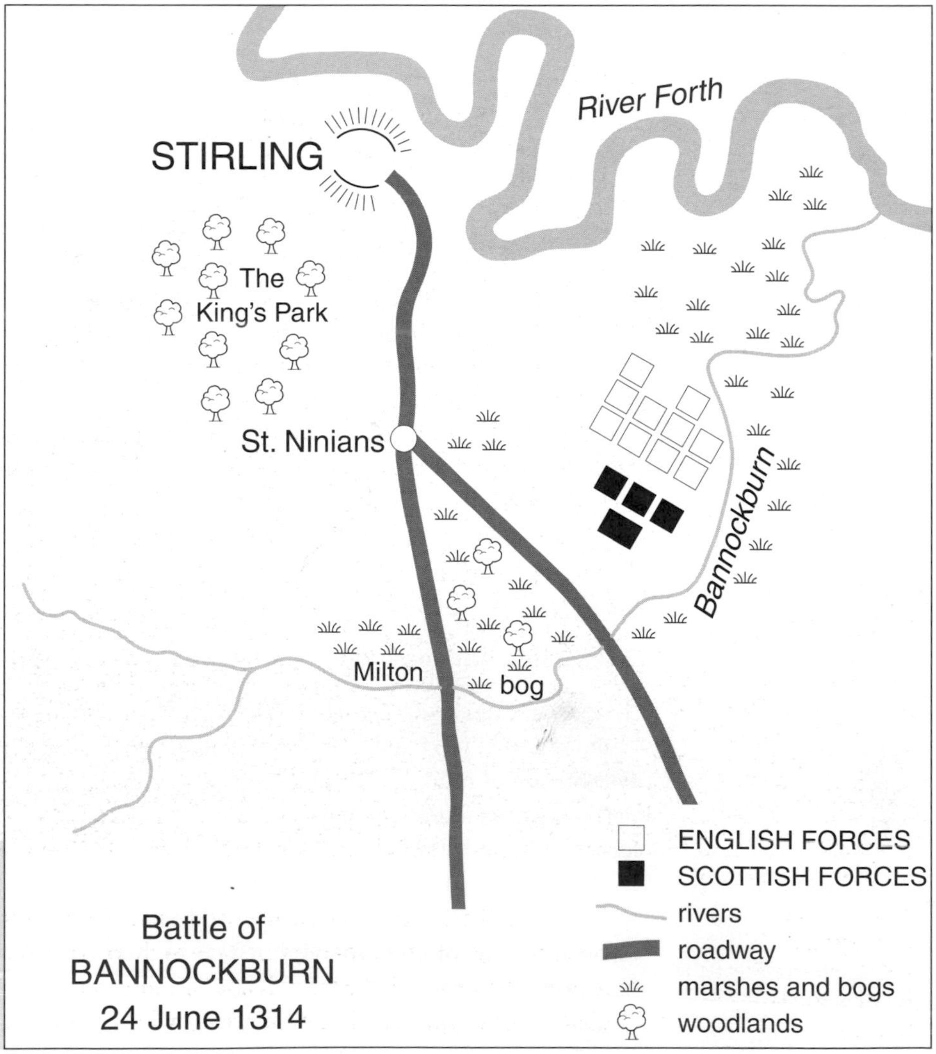

The battlefield with the burns and marshes, and the nearby River Forth, which were so skilfully used by King Robert.

STOP AND THINK

In what ways was this not a suitable battlefield for an English army that mainly used cavalry?

◆ List all the features that might have given the English army problems.

The Scots stood in four divisions, waiting for the attack. Edward II sent 800 men to relieve Stirling Castle. A smaller Scottish force led by Thomas Randolph rushed across to block their way and successfully beat off cavalry attacks. James Douglas took his men to help Randolph: a section of English troops, led by the Earls of Gloucester and Hereford, may have thought that the Scots were retreating, and chased after them. In the late evening they found, instead, that the rest of the Scottish army was moving towards them.

Sir Henry de Bohun, an English knight, recognised Bruce on the battlefield, lowered his lance and charged at him. Bruce avoided this attack and struck Sir Henry with his axe so fiercely that it broke the handle and split Sir Henry's head in two. This late evening fighting brought much heavier losses to the English forces and resulted in the advanced section of the English army retreating.

The King's skill and courage were displayed by his killing of the English knight Sir Henry de Bohun.

The main battle took place the next day. There were exchanges of fire from archers, but the more numerous English archers were not as effective as they might have been. Bruce sent Robert Keith and his horsemen to scatter them. Once more the English troops, squeezed in by the wet land and water, had to fight in too narrow a space. They faced well-organised lines of Scots infantry, able to advance to drive back cavalry charges. A chronicler writing just a few years after the battle described it:

> *The crash of the lances, the ringing of the swords, the noise of hasty blows, the groans of the dying, the cries of the wounded seemed to split the air.*

An English chronicler wrote about 30 years after the battle:

> *When both armies engaged each other and the great horses of the English charged the pikes of the Scots like into a dense forest, there arose a terrible crash of spears broken and horses wounded to death. The English in the rear could not reach the Scots because the leading divisions were in the way. There was nothing for it but to flee. This I heard from a trustworthy person who was present. The Earl of Gloucester, Sir John Comyn, and many nobles were killed besides foot soldiers who fell in great numbers. The English had crossed the Bannockburn, now they had to re-cross it. In confusion many fell into it and many were never able to get out of it. The King and others fled. Some who were not speedy were killed by the Scots who hotly pursued them.*

Edward II had allowed a battle to take place when his army was tired and hungry, and on an unsuitable battlefield. He had found it very difficult to control his nobles. Their eagerness to launch cavalry charges against well-organised spearmen had been a disaster. Fighting had been so hemmed in by the marshy ground that many infantrymen never got past the cavalry to face the enemy. The army became so tightly packed that men who fell were often trampled to death.

Bruce's skill as a leader and the ability and bravery of his men had won an overwhelming victory. King Edward fled to Dunbar Castle and then, by ship, back home. His forces also fled from Scotland. Stirling Castle surrendered. Bruce was able to exchange valuable captives, like the Earl of Hereford, for his wife, sister and daughter. Bishop Wishart was released from an English prison. Bruce's military control of his kingdom was complete.

Practise Your Skills

Answer the questions that follow, using the sources and your knowledge as appropriate.

Source A, from an account of the death of John Comyn by the fourteenth-century English chronicler Walter of Guisborough:

'Comyn, suspecting nothing, came to Bruce with a few men. When they were speaking together in words which seemed peaceful, Bruce, suddenly, with very different words, began to accuse him of betrayal. Comyn spoke peaceably and excused himself but, as Bruce had planned, he struck him with his foot and sword ... Robert Comyn, his uncle, ran to bring him help. But Christopher Seton, who had married Bruce's sister, struck his head with his sword and he died.'

Source B, from an account of the same events by the fourteenth-century Scottish chronicler, John Fordun:

'A day was appointed for Robert Bruce and John Comyn to meet together at Dumfries. John Comyn was accused of treachery and he denied it. The evil speaker was stabbed and wounded in the church of the Friars. On being asked by those around if he would live he straightaway answered "I can"; his enemies, on hearing this, gave him another wound as he died.'

1. Compare these two accounts of the same events. (Evaluate sources – making a comparison between two sources.)
2. Why do you think these accounts differ? (Evaluate sources – taking account of the origin or purpose and context of the sources.)
3. Explain why Bruce and Comyn were so hostile to each other. (Explain historical developments and events.)

Chapter 4: An overview

Bruce

- Bruce was involved in the killing of John Comyn.
- He seized the crown.
- Some nobles and the main Church leaders backed him.
- He was defeated and was forced to escape.
- He returned and won a series of small conflicts, captured and destroyed castles.
- Growing numbers came to support him.
- He achieved control of almost all of Scotland, and was able to attack the North of England.
- He faced a huge English army at Bannockburn. By skilful tactics and brave fighting he was completely victorious.
- English control of parts of Scotland was at an end.

Bruce's enemies

- Powerful sections of Scottish society were alarmed by this upheaval. Important Scottish leaders opposed him.
- Edward I sent an army that helped the Scots to completely defeat Bruce.
- Death of Edward I: his son was not a good leader and had enemies in England.
- Scots opposed to Bruce were widely scattered and defeated one by one.
- English-held castles fell to Bruce.
- Edward II did little until forced to come to save Stirling.
- The English army was defeated and retreated from Scotland.

5 King Robert's Triumph

Key Points
This chapter looks at:
- King Robert's rule in Scotland.
- His attacks on England.
- His peace settlement with England.

King Robert's peaceful policies

Bannockburn settled who was in charge of Scotland. A chronicler of the time wrote:

> *After the victory Robert Bruce was commonly called King of Scots by all men because he had acquired Scotland by force of arms.*

Several of Bruce's former enemies, such as the Earl of March, hastily made their peace with the King. Five months after the battle Bruce held a Parliament at Cambuskenneth Abbey, Stirling. There the Parliament decided that Scots who had opposed the King and who still did not seek his pardon:

> *... should be disinherited for ever of their land and other estates within the kingdom of Scotland. And henceforth they shall be held to be enemies of the King and the kingdom.*

This was written in the Statute of Cambuskenneth which also ended the habit of some nobles of holding land in both England and Scotland. The Scots who still opposed Bruce, like the former Earl of Atholl, came to be known as 'the Disinherited' because they had lost their lands. Bruce now used their properties to reward his most loyal followers like Sir James Douglas and Thomas Randolph. Douglas lands in the Borders became very extensive.

Bruce held regular parliaments, passed laws, and tried to encourage the growth of trade and of burghs. But his position was not generally recognised outside Scotland. Edward II of England still refused to accept Bruce as King of an independent Scotland. The King of France, eager for allies against England, renewed his anti-English alliance with Scotland in the Treaty of Corbeil, 1326. The Pope, however, was not so helpful. In 1316 John XXII became Pope. He was very eager to launch a CRUSADE and tried in vain to win Scottish help. English agents encouraged the Pope to blame Bruce for wanting to continue to fight England. The Pope not only excommunicated Bruce, but did the same to four bishops who backed their King.

◆ CRUSADE – campaign by Christian forces to defeat people of another religion

It was important, therefore, for Scots to persuade the Pope that he was wrong. The most important of their efforts was a letter sent from Arbroath Abbey in 1320 in the name of 39 earls and barons with the further support of 11 other nobles. The author of the long letter is not absolutely certain, but it may have been written by Bernard, Abbot of Arbroath, who was the King's Chancellor. The letter is known as the Declaration of Arbroath.

The Declaration tried to show that:

- Scotland had been an independent kingdom for a long time.
- It had had 113 kings of its own.
- Edward I was a cruel tyrant who caused destruction and death and tried to end Scotland's freedom.
- Robert Bruce had rescued his people from misery and was rightfully now the King.
- If Bruce tried to put Scotland under English control then he would be driven out and replaced.

The Declaration ended with these words:

> ***For as long as a hundred of us are alive we will never on any conditions be subjected to the Lordship of the English. For we do not fight for glory or riches or honours, but for freedom alone, which no good man gives up except with his life.***

The Declaration was a powerful and remarkable letter. It helped a Scottish campaign that eventually persuaded Pope John to recognise Bruce as King and end his excommunication. However, Bruce also had other, more violent ways of winning recognition of his position.

Arbroath Abbey, the site of the signing of one of the greatest documents in Scottish history.

Attacking the English

The Campaigns of Robert I

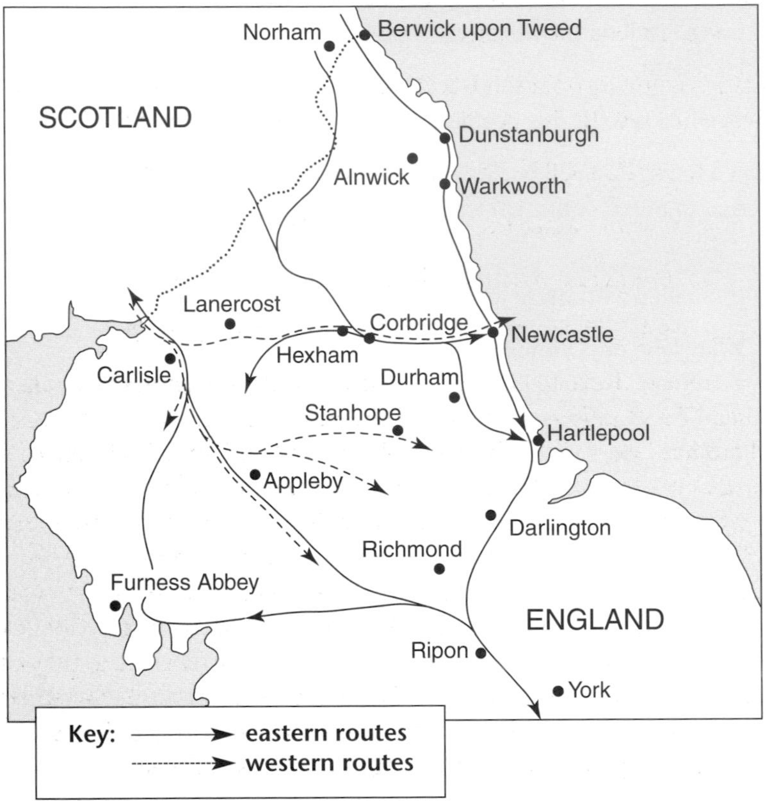

After Bannockburn England was badly led. Edward II's enemies were led, at first, by the Earl of Lancaster. In 1326 Edward's wife, Isabella, and an exiled noble, Roger Mortimer, with whom she lived, attacked Edward. Edward was captured. He had to give up his position as King in 1327. He was put in Berkeley Castle where he was horribly murdered.

Scottish soldiers were now very experienced and skilful. They often rode small horses, getting off them to fight on foot. Soldiers like these were called 'hobelars'. A French chronicler wrote, *'The Scots are tough, they cover 60 to 70 miles at a time. They live for long periods on half-cooked meat and river water. Each man carries a flat stone and a little bag of oatmeal. They put the stone on a fire and mix oatmeal and water. When the stone is hot they lay this thin paste on it and make a little cake'.*

Edward II also claimed to be Lord of Ireland. In 1315 Edward Bruce took an army there. A few Irish joined him. He defeated the Earl of Ulster and other supporters of Edward, but was finally beaten and killed in 1318. Scots recovered the Isle of Man and held it till 1333.

Bruce re-captured Berwick. He, Douglas and Randolph, led repeated raids on England that reached as far as York. They burned buildings, seized property and killed people and animals. Only Andrew Harclay seemed a skilful enough leader to fight them. He defended Carlisle from the Scots. But even he decided that, with no support from his King, he had better make peace with Bruce. For this he was condemned as a traitor. Yet when Edward's son became leader (as King Edward III) he and his advisors could not defeat the Scots.

Bruce's attacks were aimed at persuading English leaders to accept him as King of an independent Scotland. They also brought gains for Scotland, as Scots seized English property and some English places paid money to escape being attacked.

Peace at last?

The young Edward III and his advisors saw that peace was needed. Bruce proposed peace terms, and talks began in Newcastle, later moving to Edinburgh where, on 17 March 1328, peace was agreed. This Treaty of Edinburgh was accepted by the English Parliament at Northampton (historians often call it the Treaty of Northampton). The Treaty stated that:

- 'There be a true, final and perpetual peace between the Kings, their heirs and successor and their lands and subjects.'
- Bruce's heir, his four-year old son David, should have a marriage arranged with Joan, sister of Edward III: £2,000 a year should be found by Bruce for Joan.
- Bruce agreed to pay £20,000 to England, over a three-year period.
- The Scots alliance with France was to remain in place.
- Scots would not interfere in Ireland to help England's enemies.
- English Kings would not claim rights over Scotland and its people.

Bruce had wanted the Treaty to clearly say that his Scottish enemies would not get back their lands. 'The Disinherited' persuaded Edward III not to agree to this.

Bruce did not live long to enjoy his triumph. He died on 7 June 1329, aged 55. He failed to ever go on a crusade, but asked Sir James Douglas to promise to take his heart on one. Douglas fulfilled this promise, and died carrying it out on a crusade against the Moors in Spain. Bruce's remains were buried in Dunfermline Abbey.

Yet Bruce's success did not mean peace. When his son became David II, he was five years old and too young to rule properly. In 1332 Edward Balliol attacked, determined to become King. He won a great victory at Dupplin Moor, and when he got into difficulties, was backed by Edward III. English forces recovered Berwick, overwhelmed David's supporters at Halidon Hill and controlled southern Scotland. It was to be a long time before a final peace between the kingdoms was established.

The great seal of King Robert (1326) shows him as a mounted warrior.

Practise Your Skills

Answer the questions that follow, using the sources and your knowledge as appropriate.

Source A, from the early fourteenth-century English chronicle of Lanercost:

'Now after (January 1322) ... the Scottish army invaded England and marched into Durham. James Douglas and the Steward of Scotland went forward plundering the country in all directions, one of them raiding towards Hartlepool and the other towards Richmond. The people of Richmond, having no defender, bought off the invaders with a great sum of money.'

1 Explain why Scots forces attacked the North of England. (Explain historical developments and events.)

Source B, from the writings of the modern historian R. C. Paterson:

'The Treaty of Edinburgh was signed on 17 March 1328, largely on the basis of the terms put forward by King Robert. It was (agreed) by the English Parliament at Northampton on 4 May.'

2 What were the terms of this treaty? (Demonstrate knowledge and understanding of historical developments, events and issues.)

Chapter 5: An overview

King Robert secured his crown ...

At home

- His former enemies in Scotland accepted him.
- Parliament's law took lands from his Scottish enemies.
- He rewarded his followers.

With the Pope

- Scottish Bishops and nobles supported the King.
- Letters to the Pope argued the case for Scottish freedom.
- The **Declaration of Arbroath** was a very powerful argument.
- The Pope recognised Bruce as King.
- The Pope ended his excommunication.

By war

- Edward Bruce invaded Ireland.
- Scottish forces repeatedly raided the North of England.
- Scots recovered Berwick.

By peace

- Edward II was a poor leader and had enemies.
- Edward II lost his position as King.
- Edward III had to agree to peace.
- He accepted Bruce as King of an independent Scotland by the **Treaty of Edinburgh/Northampton**.

Postscript: Remembering Wallace and Bruce

Scots have been remembering Wallace and Bruce for centuries. The first great Wallace Statue was put up in 1844. Between 1861 and 1869 the great memorial to him, by the battlefield site of Stirling Bridge, was built. Now statues to both men can be found in several places in Scotland. The site of Bannockburn is overseen by the National Trust for Scotland and attracts visitors from all over the world.

The two men are remembered in poems, plays and paintings and more recently Wallace was portrayed in the film *Braveheart* by the Hollywood star Mel Gibson. Yet they lived in a country that was very different from modern Scotland. They were involved in very violent events.

One of many statues to Wallace, all showing him in heroic style.

The Wallace Monument was built in 1869 and overlooks the site where Wallace defeated the English in the Battle of Stirling Bridge.

A statue of Bruce at Bannockburn, where he triumphed over Edward II's army.

STOP AND THINK

Why do you think that Wallace and Bruce are still seen as very important?

Extended Responses

The Intermediate 2 Course requires students to produce an Extended Response. It counts for a quarter of the marks for the whole course. Your Extended Response could come from this course unit.

Always remember to:

- Find a topic in the course that especially interests you.
- Work out and discuss a question on this topic that you believe you could answer.
- Read as much as possible about it.
- Make organised notes to gather information from which to answer the question. (It will help if you can work out a list of sub-headings for your question.)
- See if you can find a few short quotes from historians and from people at the time (primary sources) to copy down.
- Make a plan of how you will answer your question. This plan must not be more than 150 words long. You may take this plan with you when you write out your full answer. It must be sent in with your full answer.
- Set out your plan so that your full answer has a general introductory paragraph, a clear conclusion and, between these, well-organised paragraphs on different parts of the answer. These should have in them the evidence to prove you have good reasons for your views.

How to choose a question

Choose a part of the course in which you are interested and about which it is fairly easy to find more to read. Some possible questions are listed below.

- Why were Scottish forces so successful at Stirling Bridge?
- How can you explain Robert Bruce's victory over a bigger English army at Bannockburn?
- Did John Balliol deserve to lose the crown?
- What made it possible for Robert Bruce to defeat his Scottish opponents?
- In what ways was the Church important at this time?
- Why did Edward I fail to win full control of Scotland?
- 'Bruce succeeded because Edward II was a very incompetent King.' Do you agree?

A possible plan
'Why were Scottish forces so successful at Stirling Bridge?'

Introduction

- The battle in outline.
- The very big scale of difference between the sides.
- The result.

Leaders

- Wallace and Murray. Their fighting experience and skill.
- Edward II's lack of interest in military affairs. Lack of proper control over army.

Armies

Scottish army
Size, balance of different parts of the army, weapons, their value, tactics. Home ground.

English army
Size, cavalry and its needs, problems and supply, arrogance of leaders.

Battlefield

River, soft ground, slope, narrow causeway, narrow bridge, who it suited.

Tactics

- Positions of two armies.
- Reasons for English recall of men and further delays.
- Failure to listen to good advice.
- Impetuous attack.

Events

Partial English crossing. Scots attack. English unable to use cavalry properly. Archers not properly used. Retreat. Bridge and river casualties.

Conclusion

- Summary of main reasons for success.
- Discussion of which reason or reasons mattered most.

Glossary

BURGH place larger than township, often local centres for merchants and craftsmen

BURGESS important man in the burgh

CHAMBERLAIN member of royal household in charge of finances from the royal lands and from burgh tolls and customs

CHANCELLOR member of the royal household who looked after the royal seal, the chapel and was a record keeper and general administrator

CHARTER a written law or statement from the king

CONSTABLE the king's chief military officer

CRUSADE campaign by Christian forces to defeat people of another religion

EXCOMMUNICATION being cast out of the Roman Catholic Church

FEUDALISM a system of duties, services, responsibilities and payments between different layers of society in western Europe during the Middle Ages

GOVERNOR The English King's representative in Scotland, controlling the country for his master

GUARDIAN a man chosen to rule the country because no adult King was available

HOMAGE acknowledgement by someone of another man as his feudal superior

JUSTICIAR a very senior official dealing with the law

LIEGEMAN subject of a feudal superior

MARSHALL member of the royal household in charge of the most expensive part of the army – the cavalry

OATH OF FEALTY a promise made on the bible to be loyal to a king or lord

OVERLORD a king who was so important that other kings or princes accepted him as having rights over them and their lands

SEABOARD land by the coast

SHERIFF a royal official responsible for a local area

STEWARD the man who managed the royal household

TREASURER in charge of Scottish money matters for Edward I

Index